DISNEY

LEARN TO DRAW

CHIP N DALE

© DISNEY

RESCUE RANGERS

Illustrated by
David Pacheco
Pattie Tomsicek
Diana Wakeman

Walter Foster

Hi, Friends!

In this book we'll show you how to draw Chip and Dale. It's lots of fun and it's easier than you'd think! You'll need to pick up a few basic supplies before we begin. Let's see what you need.

YOU'LL NEED A PENCIL TO DRAW. A NUMBER 2 IS BEST!

USE AN ERASER TO REMOVE ANY MISTAKES OR UNWANTED PENCIL LINES.

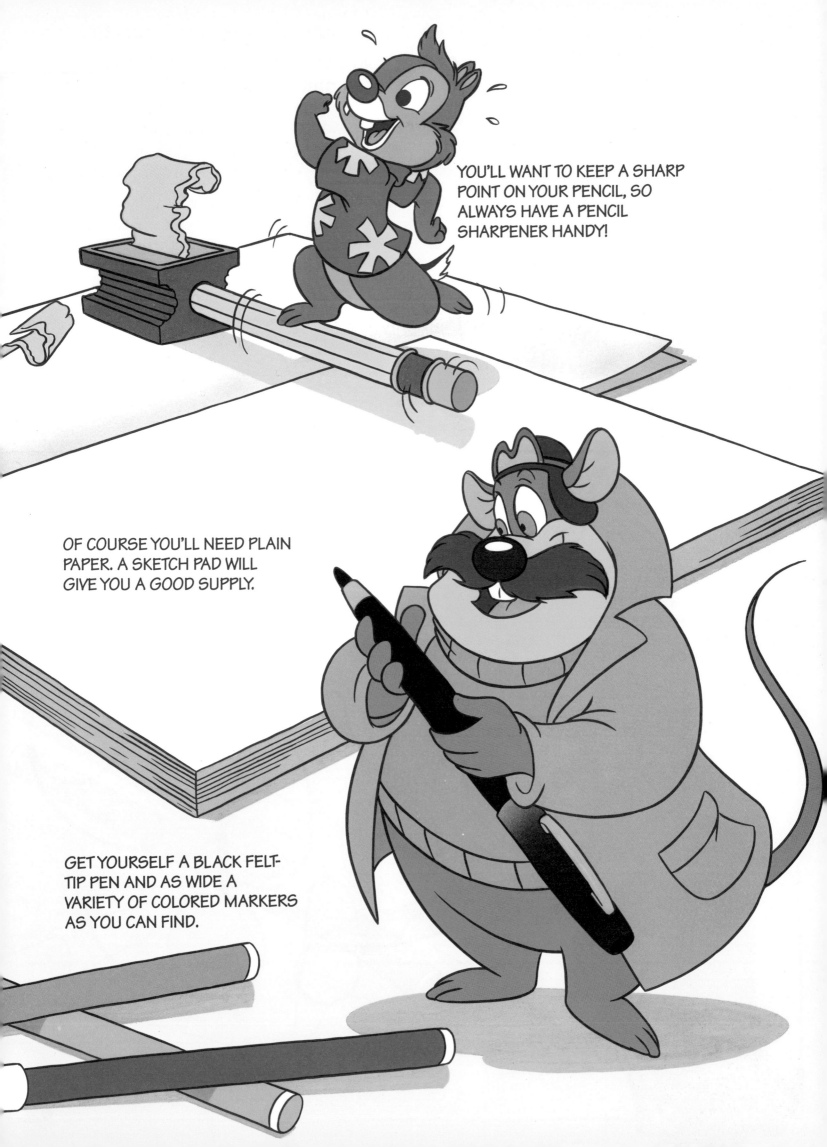

YOU'LL WANT TO KEEP A SHARP POINT ON YOUR PENCIL, SO ALWAYS HAVE A PENCIL SHARPENER HANDY!

OF COURSE YOU'LL NEED PLAIN PAPER. A SKETCH PAD WILL GIVE YOU A GOOD SUPPLY.

GET YOURSELF A BLACK FELT-TIP PEN AND AS WIDE A VARIETY OF COLORED MARKERS AS YOU CAN FIND.

Getting the Right Shapes

You can draw Chip's and Dale's faces using just a few simple shapes! Practice drawing these curved lines and shapes lightly, over and over, right on top of each other, until they look just right.

DRAW LINES WITH DIFFERENT CURVES—SMOOTH CURVES, AND SHARP ONES. DRAW LOTS OF CURVES TOGETHER.

LIGHTLY DRAW AROUND AND AROUND UNTIL NICE, ROUND CIRCLES START TO FORM. DRAW CIRCLES OF DIFFERENT SIZES.

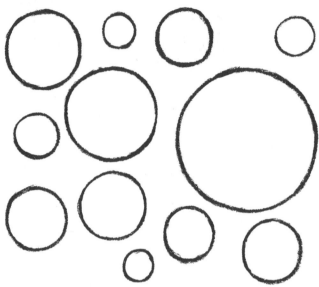

AN OVAL LOOKS LIKE A CIRCLE THAT HAS BEEN STRETCHED OR SQUASHED. DRAW OVALS OF DIFFERENT SHAPES AND SIZES.

DRAW CIRCLES AND CURVES ON TOP OF EACH OTHER. THEN JOIN THEM TO MAKE PEAR SHAPES.

Finishing Off

Say, look what's going on here! Monterey Jack, Zipper, Gadget, and Chip are demonstrating how to start a sketch of Dale and then turn it into a finished, full-color picture. Let's see how it's done!

FIRST, MONTEREY JACK USES A NUMBER 2 PENCIL TO DRAW IN THE SIMPLE SHAPES THAT START TO FORM DALE'S HEAD.

ZIPPER IS CLEANING UP THE PENCIL DRAWING, REMOVING ANY MISTAKES OR UNWANTED LINES.

CHIP DRAWS THE FINAL OUTLINE WITH A BLACK FELT-TIP PEN. ONCE THE LINES HAVE DRIED, GADGET FILLS IN THE SHAPES WITH HER COLORED FELT-TIP MARKERS.

Let's Draw Chip's Head

Chip looks as if he has acorns stuffed in his cheeks! Curved lines, ovals and a few circles are all you need to draw his face.

1 LIGHTLY DRAW A CIRCLE FOR CHIP'S HEAD. ADD CENTER LINES AS SHOWN. THIS WILL HELP YOU PUT ALL OF CHIP'S FEATURES IN THE RIGHT PLACE.

2 DRAW SMALL, POINTED OVAL SHAPES FOR THE EARS. DRAW SMALLER OVALS INSIDE. USE CURVED LINES TO FORM CHIP'S CHEEKS. NOTE THAT THE CHEEKS ARE WIDER THAN THE CIRCLE.

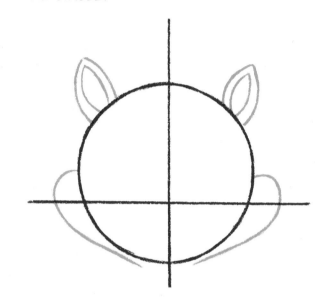

5 A CURVED LINE UNDER THE EYES MAKES THE TOP OF CHIP'S MUZZLE. ADD AN IRREGULAR OVAL FOR HIS NOSE. UNDERNEATH, DRAW HIS UPPER LIP, LOWER LIP AND TONGUE. DON'T FORGET TO ADD HIS TWO FRONT TEETH.

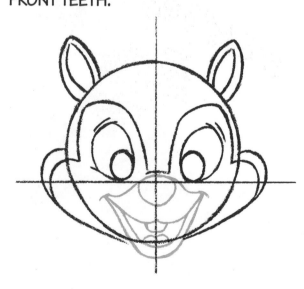

6 ADD CHIP'S HAT. DRAW THE BRIM LINE ACROSS THE TOP CURVES OF HIS EYE MASK. LET HIS EARS STICK OUT. ADD FUR TO HIS CHEEKS.

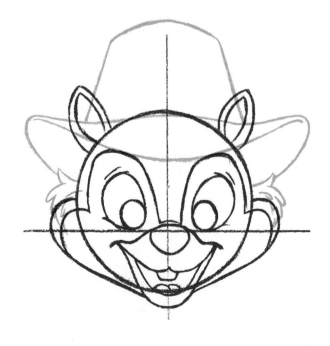

Draw each step lightly in
case you need to erase mistakes as
you go along. Remember: nobody's
perfect — not even Chip!

 3 DRAW CURVES TO FORM THE EYE AND
CHEEK MASK.

 4 DRAW OVALS WITH SMALL OVALS
INSIDE TO FORM CHIP'S EYES. A
CURVED LINE AT THE BOTTOM OF
EACH EYE ADDS FORM TO HIS CHEEK.
TO FORM THE EYELIDS ABOVE THE
EYES, DRAW SHORT, CURVED LINES.

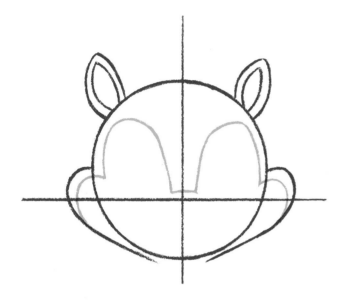

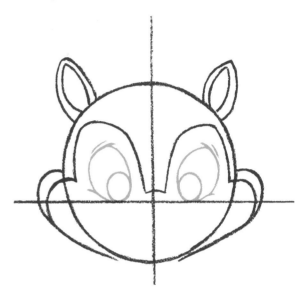

 7 DRAW A LINE ACROSS THE CROWN OF
THE HAT FOR THE HAT BAND. ADD A
VERTICAL LINE FOR THE CENTER
CREASE. ADD SHORT, CURVED LINES
ON EITHER SIDE OF CENTER LINE.
CAREFULLY ERASE ANY UNWANTED
LINES.

 8 CAREFULLY OUTLINE YOUR DRAWING
WITH INK, AND LET IT DRY. NOW COLOR
IN CHIP!

Let's Draw Dale's Head

Dale's expression always seems full of mischief. You'll need lots of sweeping curves and lines to draw his happy face.

1 LIGHTLY DRAW A CIRCLE. ADD CENTER LINES TO HELP YOU POSITION DALE'S FEATURES.

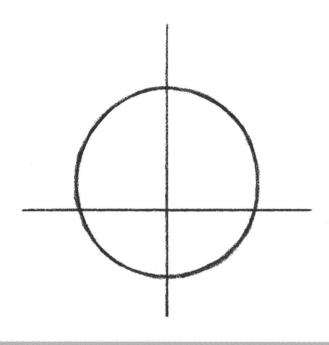

2 DRAW DALE'S EARS SO THAT THEY STICK STRAIGHT UP. MAKE SURE TO POSITION THEM CLOSE TOGETHER. USE CURVED LINES TO FORM HIS CHEEKS.

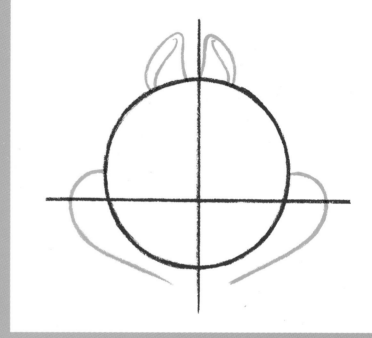

5 DRAW AN OVAL FOR THE NOSE. ADD A SMALLER OVAL HIGHLIGHT. DRAW CURVED LINES EXTENDING FROM THE NOSE TO FORM THE MUZZLE. ADD TWO TEETH SPACED WIDE APART.

6 DRAW A TUFT OF HAIR ON DALE'S FOREHEAD AND ADD FUR TO HIS CHEEKS. CURVED LINES FORM HIS LOWER LIP. ADD THE TONGUE.

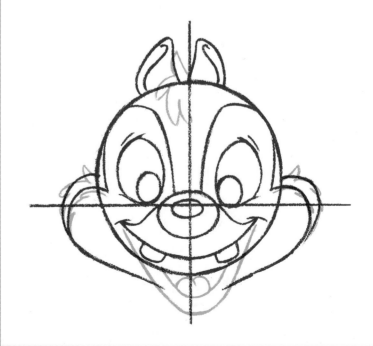

3 DRAW CURVED LINES TO FORM DALE'S EYE AND CHEEK MASK.

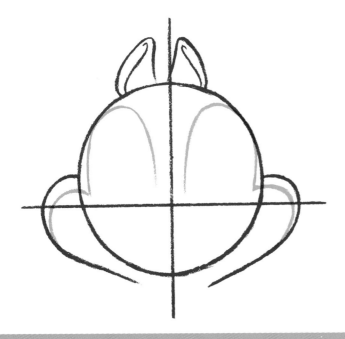

4 LARGE OVALS WITH SMALLER OVALS INSIDE WILL SHAPE THE EYES. ADD SHORT, CURVED LINES ABOVE THE EYES TO FORM EYELIDS AND BELOW THE EYES FOR ADDED SHAPE TO HIS CHEEKS.

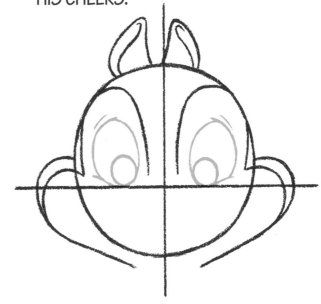

7 CAREFULLY ERASE ANY UNWANTED LINES.

8 USING INK, CAREFULLY OUTLINE YOUR DRAWING. AFTER THE INK HAS DRIED, COLOR IN DALE!

The 3/4 View — Chip

Chip thinks his 3/4 view really shows him off. This view is great for forming a variety of expressions.

1 LIGHTLY DRAW A CIRCLE. DRAW TWO CURVED CENTER LINES, ONE THAT WRAPS AROUND THE CIRCLE TOP TO BOTTOM, THE OTHER SIDE TO SIDE.

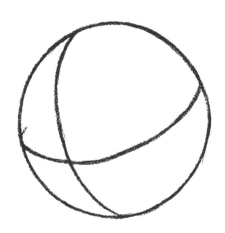

2 DRAW A SMALL OVAL ON THE RIGHT SIDE OF THE HEAD FOR THE EAR, WITH A SMALLER OVAL INSIDE. DRAW CURVED LINES TO FORM CHIP'S CHEEKS.

5 DRAW A ROUNDED TRIANGLE AT THE CENTER LINE TO FORM THE NOSE. DRAW CURVED LINES EXTENDING FROM TOP OF THE NOSE TO SHAPE CHIP'S MUZZLE. DRAW CHIP'S MOUTH WITH A CURVED LINE ATTACHED TO THE MUZZLE. ADD HIS TONGUE AND FRONT TEETH.

6 ADD THE HAT. DRAW THE BRIM ON AN ANGLE ACROSS THE TOPS OF CHIP'S EYES. DRAW A CURVED LINE NEAR THE CROWN SO THAT CHIP'S EAR CAN STICK OUT. ADD FUR TO THE CHEEKS.

3 USE CURVED LINES TO FORM CHIP'S EYE AND CHEEK MASK AND THE BRIDGE OF HIS NOSE.

4 TO FORM EYES, USE OVALS. NOTE THAT THE CLOSER EYE IS LARGER THAN THE OTHER. DRAW SHORT CURVED LINES OVER THE EYES TO FORM EYELIDS AND A CURVED LINE BELOW EACH EYE.

7 DRAW THE CREASE ON THE CROWN OF CHIP'S HAT. ADD A SMALL, CURVED LINE ON THE CROWN TO THE RIGHT OF THE CREASE.

8 AFTER YOU CAREFULLY ERASE ALL UNWANTED LINES, OUTLINE YOUR DRAWING WITH INK AND LET IT DRY. THEN COLOR IN CHIP!

The 3/4 View — Dale

Dale thinks the right side of his face has more character than the left. Let's draw a 3/4 view of his face, showing off the right side.

1 DRAW A CIRCLE VERY LIGHTLY. DRAW TWO CURVED CENTER LINES, ONE FROM TOP TO BOTTOM, THE OTHER FROM SIDE TO SIDE.

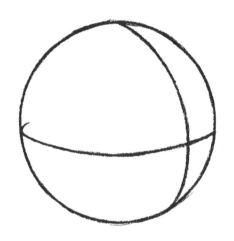

2 DRAW CURVED LINES TO OUTLINE DALE'S HEAD AND CHEEKS. TO FORM HIS EARS, DRAW TWO POINTED OVALS WITH SMALLER OVALS INSIDE, ON THE BACK OF HIS HEAD. THE CLOSER EAR SHOULD BE SLIGHTLY LARGER THAN THE OTHER.

5 SHAPE DALE'S MUZZLE WITH CURVED LINES. DRAW AN OVAL FOR THE NOSE. ADD A SMALLER OVAL FOR THE HIGHLIGHT. ADD TWO WIDELY SPACED TEETH TO THE UPPER LIP.

6 DRAW FUR ON THE CHEEKS AND FOREHEAD. COMPLETE THE MOUTH AND TONGUE WITH CURVED LINES.

3 USE CURVED LINES TO SHAPE DALE'S EYE AND CHEEK MASK, AND THE BRIDGE OF HIS NOSE.

4 OVALS WITH SMALLER OVALS INSIDE FORM DALE'S EYES. DRAW CURVED LINES OVER EYES TO SHAPE HIS UPPER LIDS. THE CLOSER EYE SHOULD BE MUCH LARGER THAN THE FARTHER ONE. ADD A CURVED LINE AT THE BASE OF THE CLOSER EYE.

7 CAREFULLY ERASE ANY UNWANTED LINES.

8 OUTLINE YOUR DRAWING WITH INK. NOW COLOR IN DALE!

Chip's Expressions

You've probably noticed that Chip's and Dale's faces are very expressive. Their moods and reactions are conveyed by stretching and squashing their flexible features.

CHIP SURE LOOKS *HAPPY* WHEN YOU SLIGHTLY TILT HIS HEAD UP, CLOSE HIS EYES, AND DRAW A WIDE, OPEN-MOUTHED SMILE.

TO CREATE A *STERN-LOOKING* CHIP, BRING THE BROWS AND EYELIDS DOWN AND ADD A SMALL, OPEN, DOWN-TURNED MOUTH.

HALF-CLOSED EYES, SLOPING BROWS, AND A SMALL, OPEN MOUTH MAKE CHIP LOOK *TIRED*.

TO MAKE CHIP LOOK *SURPRISED*, STRETCH HIS WHOLE HEAD, EYES, EARS, AND MOUTH.

LOWERING HIS BROW, SQUINTING HIS EYES, AND STRETCHING HIS DOWN-TURNED MOUTH MAKE CHIP SAY *"OUCH!"*

Let's Draw Hands

Hands are an essential part of practically all of Chip's and Dale's activities. That's why it's so important to be able to draw their hands in as many different positions as possible.

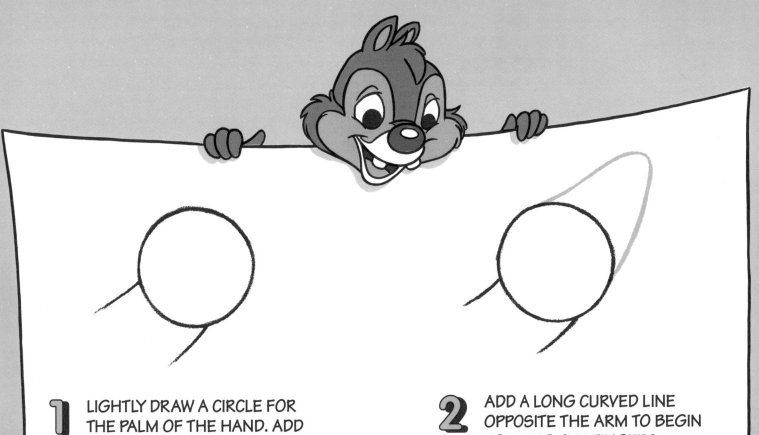

1 LIGHTLY DRAW A CIRCLE FOR THE PALM OF THE HAND. ADD TWO LINES ON THE LOWER LEFT FOR THE ARM.

2 ADD A LONG CURVED LINE OPPOSITE THE ARM TO BEGIN FORMING THE FINGERS.

3 DRAW IN TWO LONG GENTLE CURVES TO SEPARATE THE SHAPES OF THE FINGERS. USE CURVED LINES TO ADD THE THUMB. THE THUMB SHOULD BE HALFWAY BETWEEN THE FINGERS AND THE ARM.

4 ADD A CURVED PALM LINE AND REFINE THE SHAPE OF THE FINGERS. GENTLY ERASE THE CONSTRUCTION LINES AND CLEAN UP YOUR DRAWING.

Chip Standing

1

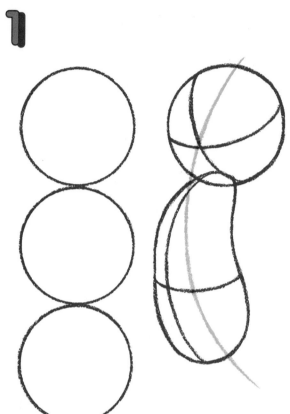

DRAW THE CURVED LINE OF ACTION. DRAW A CIRCLE FOR THE HEAD AND A PEAR SHAPE FOR THE BODY. ADD CENTER LINES TO THE HEAD AND BODY, WRAPPING THE LINES FROM TOP TO BOTTOM AND FROM SIDE TO SIDE.

2

USING THE BODY'S CENTER LINE AS A GUIDE, DRAW ONE LEG BENDING AT THE KNEE. DRAW A LARGE OPEN OVAL FOR THE OTHER LEG.

5

ADD DETAILS TO CHIP'S HANDS, FEET, AND TAIL. USE A CURVED LINE TO MARK HIS CHEST AND TUMMY. ADD FUR TO HIS CHEST AND TAIL.

6

USE CURVED LINES TO FORM CHIP'S JACKET. ADD A SERIES OF SHORT LINES AT THE WRISTS AND ALONG THE BOTTOM OF THE JACKET FOR RIBBING. DON'T FORGET THE COLLAR.

3

DRAW CURVED LINES TO FORM CHIP'S SHOULDERS AND ARMS. DRAW SMALL OVALS FOR THE HANDS AND FEET. NOTE THAT ONE FOOT POINTS TO THE SIDE, WHILE THE OTHER POINTS DOWN.

4

DRAW THE DETAILS OF CHIP'S FACE AND HAT AS YOU LEARNED BEFORE. DON'T FORGET HIS FRONT TEETH. DRAW A CURVED TRIANGLE SHAPE FOR HIS TAIL.

7

CAREFULLY ERASE ALL UNWANTED LINES.

8

GO OVER YOUR DRAWING WITH INK. NOW CHIP'S READY FOR ACTION — AND YOU'RE READY TO COLOR HIM IN!

Dale Standing

Dale is Chip's action-ready sidekick. Like his friend, Dale stands three heads high. Draw three circles the size of Dale's head.

1

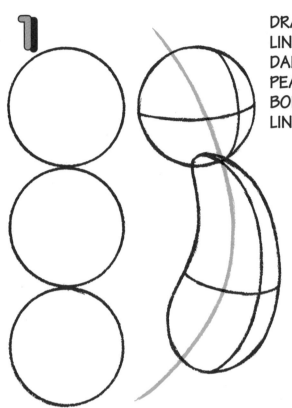

DRAW A CURVED ACTION LINE. DRAW A CIRCLE FOR DALE'S HEAD AND A PEAR SHAPE FOR HIS BODY. ADD CENTER LINES.

2

DRAW A LARGE OPEN OVAL TO FORM ONE OF DALE'S LEGS. DRAW A CURVED LINE FOR DALE'S LEFT LEG, MAKING SURE IT BENDS AT THE KNEE.

5

DRAW DETAILS OF DALE'S HANDS AND FEET. ADD A CURVED LINE TO MARK DALE'S TUMMY. ADD FUR TO HIS TAIL AND CHEST.

6

DRAW DALE'S HAWAIIAN SHIRT. NOTE THAT HIS CHEST FUR STICKS OUT.

Stack them on top of each other so that you can see how tall — or short! — Dale should be.

3

USE CURVED LINES TO DRAW DALE'S SHOULDERS AND ARMS. DRAW SMALL OVALS FOR HIS HANDS AND FEET. ONE FOOT POINTS DOWNWARD AND THE OTHER POINTS TO THE SIDE.

4

DRAW THE DETAILS ON DALE'S FACE AS YOU LEARNED BEFORE. ADD A CURVED TRIANGLE SHAPE FOR HIS TAIL.

7

GENTLY ERASE ALL UNWANTED LINES.

8

GO OVER YOUR DRAWING WITH INK. NOW CHIP'S READY FOR ACTION — AND YOU'RE READY TO COLOR HIM IN!

More Hands

It's easy to see that the hands play an important part in Chip's and Dale's actions. After you've practiced the hands that Gadget has drawn below, try making some more up on your own.

Dale's Expressions

A WIDE SMILE, RAISED CHEEKS, AND PARTIALLY CLOSED EYES MAKE DALE LOOK COY.

DALE LOOKS ANGRY WHEN YOU LOWER HIS BROW AND CHEEKS, AND ADD A SMALL, DOWN-CURVED MOUTH.

A DOWN-TURNED MOUTH AND DROOPY BROWS AND EYELIDS CREATE A VERY SAD DALE.

TO MAKE DALE LOOK *FRIGHTENED*, STRETCH HIS WHOLE HEAD, EYES, EARS, AND HAIR, TOO!

DALE LOOKS *CURIOUS* WHEN YOU GIVE HIM A SMALL, ROUND MOUTH, RAISE HIS BROWS, AND STRETCH HIS EYES.

Dale Walking Chip Running

1

LIGHTLY DRAW DALE'S LINE OF ACTION. DRAW A CIRCLE FOR HIS HEAD AND A PEAR SHAPE FOR HIS BODY. USE CURVED LINES TO FORM HIS CHEEKS, ARMS, LEGS, AND TAIL. ADD OVALS FOR HIS HANDS, FEET, AND EARS.

2

DRAW DETAILS OF DALE'S FACE AS YOU LEARNED BEFORE. ADD FUR TO HIS TAIL AND A CURVED LINE TO MARK HIS TUMMY.

1

DRAW CHIP'S LINE OF ACTION IN THE OPPOSITE DIRECTION. DRAW A CIRCLE FOR HIS HEAD AND A PEAR SHAPE FOR HIS BODY. DRAW CHEEKS, ARMS, LEGS, AND TAIL USING CURVED LINES. USE OVALS TO FORM HIS HANDS, EAR, AND FEET.

2

DRAW CHIP'S FACE AND HAT AS YOU LEARNED BEFORE. NOTE THAT CHIP'S MOUTH IS WIDE OPEN. USE CURVED LINES TO GIVE HIM A DETERMINED EXPRESSION. ADD A CURVED LINE TO FORM HIS LOWER TORSO. ADD FUR TO HIS TAIL.

3

DRAW DALE'S SHIRT.
DRAW THE DETAILS OF
HIS HANDS AND FEET.
ADD FUR TO HIS CHEST.

ERASE UNWANTED
LINES, INK AND COLOR.

4

3

USE CURVED LINES TO
DRAW CHIP'S JACKET.
ADD DETAILS TO HIS
HAND AND FEET. SHAPE
THE COLLAR TO EXTEND
ABOVE HIS CHEEKS.

ERASE UNWANTED
LINES, INK AND COLOR
IN — BEFORE CHIP
GETS AWAY!

4

Action Poses

Chip and Dale are two very active chipmunks! You'll want to be able to draw them in a wide variety of poses. Always start with a dynamic line of action.

YOU CAN FEEL THAT DALE IS POISED FOR ACTION BY THE WAY THAT HE LEANS FAR FORWARD AND HAS HIS FRONT LEG RAISED. IT LOOKS AS IF HE'S JUST SPOTTED AN ACORN!

THE LINE OF ACTION THROWS DALE'S ENTIRE BODY BACK AND UP IN MIDAIR. THIS OFF-BALANCE POSE CONVEYS A VERY STARTLED REACTION!

THE FORWARD MOVEMENT OF DALE'S BODY, COUPLED WITH HIS BACKWARD GLANCE, TELLS YOU THAT DALE IS REALLY MAKING TRACKS TO AVOID SOMETHING!

This will help you to exaggerate the movement, giving your characters maximum vitality. And don't forget to give their faces lively expressions, as well!

NOTICE HOW THE DYNAMIC LINE OF ACTION SETS CHIP'S BODY LUNGING FORWARD IN THIS EXCITING POSE.

THE LONG BOUNCY CURVES IN THIS DRAWING OF CHIP CONVEY A JOYFUL, HAPPY-GO-LUCKY FEELING.

THE FORWARD SWEEP OF CHIP'S BODY IS ESTABLISHED AT THE OUTSET BY THE LINE OF ACTION IN THIS DRAMATIC DRAWING.

Coloring Tips

CHIP AND GADGET HAVE THE RIGHT IDEA! THEY ARE USING LONG, LOOSE, DIAGONAL STROKES TO ADD COLOR TO THIS LARGE PORTRAIT OF DALE. THEY MOVE THEIR MARKERS QUICKLY AND LIGHTLY TO KEEP THE COLOR FROM COLLECTING IN DARK "PUDDLES" OR SOAKING INTO THE PAPER BEYOND THE OUTLINES.

DALE HAS SUGGESTED AN ENTIRE
WORLD AROUND CHIP BY SIMPLY
ADDING A FEW TUFTS OF GRASS
AT HIS FEET. YOUR DRAWINGS HOLD
MUCH MORE INTEREST WHEN YOU
INCLUDE A SETTING FOR YOUR
CHARACTERS!

Other Media

As you become more and more comfortable drawing Chip and Dale, you may want to experiment with some different materials to add color to your pictures. A few possibilities are shown below.

DALE'S REALLY "GETTING INTO" HIS POSTER PAINTS, ISN'T HE? YOU MIGHT ENJOY USING SOME YOURSELF.

GADGET'S DEFINITELY "GOT THE POINT" AS SHE USES COLORED PENCILS TO ADD THE FINISHING TOUCHES TO HER DRAWING. WHY DON'T YOU GIVE SOME COLORED PENCILS A TRY?

ZIPPER APPEARS TO "HAVE A HANDLE" ON THE WATERCOLORS HE'S USING TO COMPLETE HIS PICTURE OF DALE. LOOKS LIKE FUN, DOESN'T IT?